ADYAR PAMPHLETS
No. 13

Elementary Lessons on Karma

BY

ANNIE BESANT

Theosophical Publishing House
Adyar, Madras, India

ADYAR PAMPHLETS

No. 13

Elementary
Lessons on Karma

BY

ANNIE BESANT

March 1912
(Reprinted : August 1919)

THEOSOPHICAL PUBLISHING HOUSE

ADYAR, MADRAS, INDIA

Elementary Lessons on Karma

FEW questions, perhaps, puzzle students more, whether the students be old or young, than that of Karma. What is it? when did it begin? how far does it limit us? are we its servants or its masters? must we fold our hands meekly before it, or struggle vigorously against it? if to-day grows out of yesterday, and yesterday out of the day before, and so on, backwards and backwards, how can the bad man ever become good? are we not really compelled by an iron necessity, are we not "dumb, driven cattle," who cannot become heroes, whatever poets may say?

We may spend a little time usefully in thinking over these questions and others resembling them, for here, as elsewhere, " a little knowledge is a dangerous thing". Karma is but too often a crippling fetter instead of being, as it ought to be, a strength, a guide, a force, enabling us to act wisely and well. Like all other laws in nature, it binds the ignorant and gives power to the wise.

Here is our first step: Karma is a Law of Nature. We might go further, and say: It is *the* law. For it is everywhere and always—omnipresent, all-pervasive. Other names are given to it in the West, and the names are useful, because they are not surrounded by all the traditions and discussions which blur the meaning of karma in the East. The Western philosopher calls it " The Law of Causation ". He

sees in every happening a double fact—it is both
an effect and a cause; it is an effect, for it has
a cause; something went before and made this
thing to happen; it is also a cause; for it will
generate a new happening, another thing will
arise from it. As a man is a son of his father, and is
also the father of his son; as his father was a son to
his own father, and as his son will be a father to his
own son in turn, so is it with causes and effects; each
event is at once an effect and a cause—an effect of
the past, a cause of the future. This observed
succession, this invariable relation, is generalised
under the term, the law of causation. The human in-
tellect recognises this law as fundamental, and sees in
it the assurance of stability and order as well as of
human progress.

We are continually causing effects, unconscious-
ly and consciously. The more we understand our
power and nature's conditions, the more can we
bring about the effects we desire, and prevent the
events we dislike.

The Western scientist calls karma, "The Law of
Action and Re-action," and he also sees it as a fundamental law. "Action and Re-action are equal and
opposite," he says. You push an object; its resist-
ance is its re-action against your push; you fling an
elastic ball against a board; it springs back to you
with a force proportional to that of the impact.
Everywhere in nature he finds this law, and he counts
on it with certainty in his manipulations of objects.

In both these Western terms the word "Law"
appears. What is a Law—a Law of Nature? It is
the statement of an observed succession, of an invariable sequence; it may be put as a formula; wherever
A and B are, there C follows. Hence it is a statement of conditions, and the result which arises from

them. It is not a *command*; it does not say : " Do this," or " Do not do this," like a human enactment. It does not say : " You must have A and B, and therefore C ; " but rather : " If you want C, you must bring A and B together ; if you do not want C, you must take care that A and B do not come together ; if you keep A away from B, you will not have C." Hence a law of nature is truly said to be not a compelling but an enabling force ; it tells you the conditions which enable you to produce or avoid a particular thing, and is only compulsory in this sense, that *if* you make the conditions you *must* have the result. Because of this inevitable sequence ignorant people are helpless in the grip of natural laws ; they ignorantly produce conditions, and the results hurtle around them, confuse and crush them. As we gain knowledge, we take care as to the conditions we produce, and thus avoid undesirable results.

A law of Nature is said to be inviolable, for this relation between cause and effect cannot be altered. We can disregard natural laws as much as we please, but the law breaks us ; we do not break it. If you slip off the top of a building and fall heavily to the ground, you do not break the law of attraction, or gravitation ; you disregard it, and your fall proves its truth ; a well known formula gives the velocity with which you will strike the ground.

We partly answer, then, our first question, " what is karma ? " by the statement : karma is a law of nature of universal validity, called in the West the law of causation, or the law of action and re-action.

The remainder of the answer to the question, " what is karma ? " is very closely connected with the second question : " When did karma begin ? " A general law of nature cannot be said to have either a beginning, or an ending ; wherever there is any manifestation, any universe, any world, there, general laws are also present, inherent in the very nature of things. Attraction of one mass of matter to another cannot be said to *begin* ; wherever there are masses of matter, there, attraction is working ; gravitation does not *begin*, it is ever manifested where the conditions for its working are present. Hence karma, being a general Law, is said to be eternal ; it is a condition of manifested existence, and wherever existence is manifested, there is karma.

Hence the question : " When did karma begin ? " shows a misconception of the very nature of karma ; it is a perpetual condition of existence in matter, neither beginning nor ending, but eternal. If the form of the question be modified, and it is asked : " When did the karma of a particular creature begin ? " then the answer is : " At the time at which that particular creature came into manifestation." When the unborn, undying Spirit takes to himself a vesture of matter, then he steps into conditions, and comes under the law of karma. His stepping into the conditions begins his particular karma. At first it will be the karma of a mineral, the play upon him of surrounding force and matter, and the re-action from him on his surroundings. These actions and re-actions weave the links of his karma, and the chain draws him into one or another type of the vegetable kingdom. In that, as his re-action becomes more complex, the web of karma attaching to him becomes more complicated, and ultimately lifts him into some animal type. In the animal kingdom his increasing sentiency enters into kārmic causes, and pains inflicted by him re-act as pains on him. But the feeling of pain is due to the evolution of the power to feel in him ; it is still action and re-action, but where in the mineral these were unaccompanied by feeling, in the animal, feeling results in pleasure and pain : the law is the same ; the creature is different, and so the result on the creature is different. As reason develops, another stand is added to the kārmic web, and the action in the thought world is added to that in the acting and feeling worlds, and hence another powerful factor is added to the re-action. But once again, the law of action and re-action is working on the same lines.

If the student will constantly bear in mind that karma is action and re-action, and that this works on every plane of nature, works everywhere and always, and is inherent in the nature of things, many of his difficulties will disappear ; he will understand that karma begins for him when he descends into the universe of matter, because he has come into the conditions in which karma is perpetually working, and that the re-actions on him are exactly equal to his actions, containing more or fewer factors according to those which have gone out from himself.

Another thing that will become clear to him is that the re-action must be of the same nature as the action ; hence when a man commits a mistaken act with a good motive, his action is on three planes, the physical, the astral and the mental ; the re-action must also be on three planes ; the mental re-action will be on his character, which will be improved by the impact of good upon it ; the astral re-action will make for him future opportunity of exercising right desire ; both these will be good ; but the re-action upon the physical plane of the mistaken act will be misfortune to himself. Thus the law works with perfect accuracy and inviolability, and the re-action upon each action follows in unvarying succession.

The idea of rewards and punishments ought not to be allowed to enter into the workings of kārmic law. We have results, consequences, but neither rewards nor punishments. Pain is the outcome of wrong activity on any plane, not because anyone inflicts pain upon us as a punishment, but because we have flung ourselves against the law and are bruised against its unyieldingness. The result of virtuous thought or feeling is an increase of the capacity to be virtuous; it is not prosperity, either in this world or another. If we tell a lie, the result is the increased tendency to falsehood, the lowering of our character, and this is an invariable result, not affected by the discovery or otherwise of our falsity by those around us; their want of trust is the re-action from their discovery of our lie; the re-action on us of the increased tendency to falsehood is independent of this secondary result.

" How far does the law of karma limit us ? "—such is the question now to be considered, and it falls naturally into two parts: (1) The limiting action of laws of nature, of which karma is one; (2) The limiting action of the special karma which each one of us has generated in the past.

1. We have already seen that a law of nature is a sequence of conditions, and the conditions among which we find ourselves impose upon us certain limitations. Thus a man cannot fly under ordinary conditions, and if he desires to travel through the air he must supply himself with some apparatus by which he can rise into the air and move therein. The more we know of the natural forces around us, the greater is our freedom of movement amongst them, for we can balance one against the other, neutralising those which are opposed to any course which we wish

to take. If we wish to descend from a tower to the ground by jumping from the top, the conditions are such as to result in the fracture of our bones if we merely jump into the air; but if we arm ourselves with a parachute of sufficient size, we may safely launch ourselves into the air, and float gradually down to the earth. Again, we cannot rise above the atmosphere, and long before reaching its upper regions we should find the air too rare to be respirable; here is a limiting condition; but, on the other hand, we could overcome this limitation by taking with us a supply of respirable air. The power of natural conditions to limit us can very largely be overcome by knowledge, and the larger our knowledge the more freely can we act. Exactly the same is true with regard to the universal conditions called karma; we are limited by them as by the other conditions found in nature, but can neutralise or transcend these to a great extent by knowledge. Hence the enormous importance of studying and understanding the general kārmic conditions, since our freedom is proportionate to our knowledge.

2. Of more pressing and immediate importance is the limiting action of the special karma which each one of us has generated in the past, and an understanding of this is vital for the welfare of our life and the control of our conduct. This understanding will best be gained by a study of the working of karma along the three lines of character, opportunity and circumstances, generated by the three aspects of consciousness—thought, desire, and activity. In the whole of this study it must be remembered that we, who created this karma by our thought, desire and activity in the past, are the same thinking, desiring and acting consciousness in the present; people think too much of karma as reaction on them, and not

sufficiently of their own action upon kārmic conditions; we modify the outcome of past thinkings by present thinking, of past desires by present desire, of past actings by present acting. Kārmic action is not on an inert wall, but on a living consciousness, which reacts on karma and modifies it by that reaction. The passive endurance of karma is seen, and not the active impact upon it; thus a one-sided and inadequate view is taken, and man is paralysed when he ought to be energising.

An examination of each of the lines above-mentioned will enable us clearly to see how far karma limits us.

Thought makes character, such is the familiar and true statement. "As a man thinks, so he becomes." The character built up by thought in past lives is born with us in the present life. That we cannot escape, and it is a clear limitation. Let us say that we are born with poor mental abilities; these limit our capacity for acquiring knowledge, and we find ourselves compelled to spend two or three hours in mastering a lesson that our clever neighbour learns in ten minutes. There is a fact, a limitation, which undoubtedly exists. How can we deal with it? For the present we acquiesce in the fact; it is our karma. But, if we know the law, we shall at once begin to exercise our faculties, such as they are, to the full : we shall exert ourselves to the utmost, making up in time what we lack in power. Gradually the limits begin to widen out; thought is exerting its creative power, and our faculties improve under our strenuous cultivation. Accepting the limitation imposed by our poor thinking in the past, we sedulously work at its extension by better thinking now, and thus build up gradually an improved mental equipment for use in the future. Or we may have

been born with an irritable temper; contrasting
ourselves with a sweet-tempered neighbour, we are
keenly conscious of our inferiority; again we feel our
kārmic limitation. But again we decline to sit down
passively within it; we determinedly think patience,
until at last we have created it as a faculty, and it
becomes our habitual self-expression. Karma may
hand on to us our wages for the past in the form of
limitations, but karma cannot keep us within that
area if we resolutely determine to break them down;
within those limits we must begin, but we can change
them by the very force which created them.

Desire makes opportunity; such is the second familiar
law. We may have been born clever, but opportunity to show our ability may be lacking; or we may
make efforts which fail of success through " bad luck "
rather than through defective workmanship. Clearly
we are here hemmed in by a limitation; karma is
frustrating our endeavours. Here, again, we must
meet the limitation by resistant and persevering effort;
we must back up our effort by strong desire, and
will the success which eludes our grasp. Gradually
we shall create opportunities and conquer our fate,
and the limitations will widen out and the obstacles
disappear.

Action makes circumstances is the third law. Most
difficult of all are the limitations imposed by circumstances; but these also may slowly be changed. The
best way is to accept them cheerfully and bravely,
adapting ourselves within the limitations from which
at first we cannot escape, but keeping up against them
a quiet steady pressure, which slowly modifies them.
Above all, we should try to increase the happiness of
those around us, thinking little of our own, for past
selfishness has made present misfortune, and the
changing of the cause will bring about a changed

effect. Within the present evil we sow the seed of future good, and within the limitations made by the past we create freedom for the future.

We will next consider the bearing on this question of Bhīṣhma's famous phrase : " Exertion is greater than Destiny."

Past exertions have made present destiny, present destiny may be changed by fresh exertions. A study of the conditions of such changing will complete our answer to the question : " How far does the law of karma limit us ? "

We have seen that "thought makes character". We look at our own character, and we see that we are deficient in truth, courage and gentleness. How shall we supply this deficiency since it is our karma to be untruthful, timid, and irritable. Thought is our tool for building up what we lack. Every morning we sit down quietly for five minutes and we think about truth. We say to ourselves : "Truth is Brahman; everything rests on truth. In my real Self I am truth, for I am divine. My mind, my body, must express my real Seif. To-day, I will think truthfully and accurately. I will say nothing untrue. I will do nothing that makes a false impression. O Thou who art Truth, and art my Self, shine out in me as Truth, and help me to be true." Then, during the day, we try to be on our guard against thinking, speaking, or acting untruthfully.

If we exaggerate anything, our morning thought will come up in the mind, and we shall at once feel that we have been untruthful. In such a case, we should deliberately and openly correct the false statement, though we shall feel a little bit ashamed of ourselves in doing so, and this will make us more careful next time. Thus we should go on, day after day, week after week, until we have established a habit of truthfulness in thought, word and deed, and we find, to our delight, that we are instinctively truthful, and the deficiency has vanished, the virtue of truth is ours.

Then we begin, all over again, to build up courage. We think about it in the morning, we practise it during the day. When we feel timid we say to ourselves: " Brahman is fearless, my Self is fearless; my mind and body must be brave." We read about brave people, and dwell on the value of courage. If we see a child or an animal ill-used, we do not slink out of the way, and say : " It is not my business." We go boldly up, and speak gently but firmly to the cruel person, and try to protect the helpless creature he is ill-using. After a time we find that timidity has disappeared, and we have become courageous.

Then we begin again once more to substitute gentleness for irritability; we think on gentleness every morning, we practise it during the day. If a person speaks to us sharply, and our irritable temper starts up all aflame, we force ourselves to be silent, not to answer back ; when we can do this without effort, then we begin to answer gently, to soothe the ruffled feelings of the other, until at last we can bear any annoyance without impatience or irritation.

Another very good way of thinking in the morning, is to imagine ourselves perfectly truthful, or perfectly brave, or perfectly gentle. The imagination creates, and we become the model of the virtue which we have imagined ourselves to be. We think of ourselves as the " very perfect knight," truthful, brave and gentle, and we become that which we think. By this use of the law of thought we have created new karma, and it has become our karma to be truthful, courageous, gentle. We have established this as our settled character, and we shall be born with it when we return to earth next time. Karma may compel us to bring with us into the world a nature which is untruthful, timid and irritable, but it cannot compel us to keep that nature. We *can* what we *will*, and karma will give a truthful, brave and gentle nature, if we set going the causes which produce it ; karma is merely result, and as the one character is the inevitable result of certain causes, so is the other character the equally inevitable result if we choose to set going the appropriate causes.

We have seen that "desire makes opportunity". We think carefully and quietly of the things which will be really useful to us, choosing the more permanent as against the less permanent, the intellectual and emotional as against the physical. Then we deliberately set ourselves to desire the most desirable objects. We desire them steadily, perseveringly, and we watch for the opportunities which our desire is making for us, and seize them as they present themselves. But let us remember that the law works unswervingly, and that we shall inevitably find falling into our hands the opportunity we have resolutely created, bringing with it the desired object. If ill-chosen, it will bring disappointment not satisfaction, sorrow not joy. Nature pays over results, indifferent to their nature, and it is for us to choose as we will. Hence the warning : " Take heed how ye pray."

We have seen also that " action makes circumstances," and that we lie in beds of our own making. A careful consideration of the relation between our character and our circumstances will teach us how best we may utilise the environment from which we cannot escape. While we diligently try to spread happiness round us, we should take advantage of the conditions to develop qualities we lack. From ill-health we may cull the sweet flowers ot cheerfulness and patience; from household cares we may learn tenderness, and develop executive ability; from the drudgery of daily toil we may learn endurance; from anxiety we may evolve fortitude and serenity. The knower of karma turns everything to account and, like a strong and skilful workman, he shapes his future. Karma conditions us, but we are its creators, and in proportion to our knowledge is our control.

The little group of questions remaining is really answered in essence by what has been said, but we may run over certain additional details. " Are we the servants of karma, or its masters ? Must we fold our hands meekly before it, or struggle vigorously against it ? If to-day grows out of yesterday, and yesterday out of the day before, and so on, backwards and backwards, how can the bad man ever become good ? are we not really compelled by an iron necessity ? "

The first question of this group we may pass as already answered : we are partly servants, partly masters—servants by what remains in us of ignorance, masters by all the powers we gain by knowledge. The second question, however, raises an important point. Suppose we find ourselves in the grip of an overwhelming force and any struggle against it is doomed to failure, is there any use in struggling ? Every use, as a little thought will show. Let us take a bad physical habit, brought over from the past— drunkenness or sexual sensuality. The man who does not understand karma, says despairingly : " I cannot help it," and he yields without a struggle, and thus weaves another strand into the rope of vice that binds him, making it stronger than before. The man who understands karma says : " It may be that

I cannot help it, but I am going to fight against it for as long as I can, even if I have to succumb in the end." He makes a gallant fight against his enemy ; beaten at last by the overwhelming force of his past, he sinks again into the vice ; but his noble struggle has broken many strands of that strong rope of evil karma, and when again his foe assails him, the rope will bind him less securely, and he will be able to make a better fight, until—even though it be after many struggles and many defeats—the rope will snap, his limbs will be free, and he will slay his enslaver. When a man has created a vice by evil desire, evil thought, and evil act, he, its creator, can also be its destroyer, by good desire, good thought, and good act. Thread by thread the rope of karma is twisted ; thread by thread the rope of karma may be untwisted ; none but man himself creates his destiny, " none else compels ". Take courage, then, all ye who find your present tied and bound by your past ; fear not, be of good courage, exert to the very utmost all the strength you have ; and you shall inevitably free yourselves, and stand erect as masters where now you crawl as slaves. For law is law, and by the same law by which we bound ourselves shall we now assuredly free ourselves ; the law remains the same, and that which in ignorance we wrought by it shall we now through knowledge undo by it, and none can say us nay.

The third question of this group is one which often seems to disturb the mind of the student ; must not a vicious man, who continues to live viciously, come back in another life yet more vicious, and so on and on ? There are certain counteracting forces which have to be considered. In the first place unhappiness follows on vice, to some extent in this world, to a

great extent in the next. The drunkard, the sensu-
alist, develop a bloated, coarsened body, with shaken
nerves and ruined health. How often may such an
one be heard to regret his folly, and to declare that if
he could live his life over again, he would live it
differently. Experience teaches, in spite of our
wilfulness, and the disregarded law bruises the evil-
doer. The suffering grows keener on the other side
of death, as the scorpion of evil desire stings its
nurturer, and the man is forced to recognise that he
is living in a world of law, where he may dash himself
against the barriers but cannot break them. When
he passes from the intermediate world into the
heavenly, every seed of good he has within him grows
into flower ; all that there is of pure and loving in him
develops and increases : when the heaven-life is over,
the good side of him is strengthened, his faculties are
improved. On his return to earth he also brings with
him the result of his sad experience as a shrinking
from the evil in which before he delighted. The
memory of suffering endured, burnt into the soul, has
become a cause for avoidance of the evil which induc-
ed it, and thus, by the action of law, is a change
brought about in the attitude of the man towards
that particular vice. Again, humanity as a whole is
slowly carried forward in the great current of evolution, and the evil-doer is carried with it, though he
may retard his own progress, almost to the point of
stationariness ; but this wilful setting of a part
against the whole, the insolent setting of the indivi-
dual will against the universal, causes a friction that
becomes intolerably painful, and at last ceases by the
strong compulsion of this pain. Or again, the evil-
doer reads a book, hears a discourse, meets a
person, that arouses in him a recognition of the
folly of the course he is pursuing, opens his
eyes to the suffering he is creating for himself,

16

and stirs his intelligence and his will into an effort to change. Or again, the disapproval of those he loves and honours, the wish to gain affection instead of incurring dislike, these act upon him as a new cause to cease from evil and to do good. Or yet again, the mere fact of his own growth, the unfolding, however slow, of the divine Spirit which is his deepest Self, inevitably quickens the inborn tendency to good and causes a struggle against evil. Man's tendency is upwards not downwards, and only by doing violence to his own nature can a man grovel in a dust-heap instead of walking with face uplifted to the sun.

"Are we not really compelled by an iron necessity?" There is but one necessity which binds the universe—the loving Will of its Emanator to raise it to perfection and bliss. As God's very Life is the life in His worlds, that Life lifts them ever to higher and fuller expression of Beauty, of Good, of Happiness. Evolution is the essence of that Will, and sooner or later, as the magnetised needle sets itself to the Pole, so must man's will set itself to the divine, whereof it is indeed a part. Man is at strife with himself, and hence the turmoil and the pain. When he sees his lasting happiness, the substance instead of the shadow, then will he be at one with himself and one with Divinity, and enter into the Peace.

———

Printed by J. R. Aria at the Vasanta Press, Adyar, Madras.

THE ADYAR PAMPHLETS

Vol. IX.

Annual Subscription : Re. 1-8 or 2s. or 50c.   *Postage Free.*
Single Copy : As. 2 or 2d. or 4c.   *Postage Extra.*

.Theosophical Publishing House, Adyar, Madras

CPSIA information can be obtained
at www.ICGtesting.com
Printed in the USA
BVHW032051230121
598417BV00013B/7